Sensei-tional!
Confessions of English Teachers in Japan

by Rex Chesney

Sensei-tional!
February 2008
First Edition

All rights reserved
Copyright © 2008 by Rex Chesney

ISBN 978-1-4357-0996-6

Introduction

While there are a small number of English teachers in Japan committed to moulding minds, the vast majority are horny and hedonistic young travellers desperate to delay their adulthood by drinking as much as is humanly possible and shagging anything with a pulse. These marauding delinquents have visa stamps in their passports which say "specialist in humanities and international relations," but they're about as deserving of them as the Vikings.

You see, Japan is a fun and fascinating place to be, from its ancient temples to its psychedelic games arcades and karaoke bars, but it's also hugely expensive, so those who want to visit usually need an employment visa to help fund their shenanigans which, unless you're bilingual or sexy enough to be a model, means but one option – teaching English.

Fortunately there are several huge corporations who'll hire any chancer with the right accent, and you don't even need teaching skills to get the gig. There are two main job choices for the unqualified teacher in Japan. Firstly, you can work in an "Eikaiwa," instructing small groups of adults in the art of English conversation. This job is often misinterpreted by new teachers as chatting for a living- the perfect way for aspiring Lenos and Lettermans to hone their interviewing technique. But don't worry if you have the conversational skills of Harpo Marx, they'll probably hire you anyway.

 Alternatively, you could be an assistant language teacher in a junior-high or high school, helping out a local teacher by standing around looking goofy and performing the functions of a tape-recorder.

 Both of these are extremely easy jobs and, particularly if you are an attention-starved nerd, the knowledge that people are actually paying to hear you speak is good for the self-esteem.

AT HOME

IN JAPAN

And so, year after year, hordes of recently-graduated party animals arrive in small towns throughout Japan, and come to be known locally as "Sensei," (which, for those who haven't seen "The Karate Kid," is Japanese for "teacher,") even though some of these "teachers" are so inept they should be sued under the trade descriptions act for calling themselves such.

Irregular verbs and past-participles are of little concern to the average newcomer. Most would guess that "verb-conjugation" is a sexually-transmitted disease. With endless parties to attend, sights to see, and exotic girls and guys to pursue, these teachers often resent the work getting in the way of their fun. It's hard to adapt to the Japanese workaholic-ethic when your job is simply an excuse to prolong your adolescence. Reckless young teachers saunter into work hungover, nod off in class, or call in sick twice weekly. They blithely trash their company apartments and hop into bed with their adult students at every available opportunity. In a country famous for it diligent and dutiful workforce, this devil-may-care attitude often leads to colossal culture clashes.

It's such antics that I have chronicled in this book. True tales of debauchery and drunkenness, that I've witnessed first-hand, been told by friends or, I'm afraid to say, committed myself.

In my several years of working for various language schools in Japan, I've seen dozens of teachers come and go, and every week I hear fresh confessions from the latest recruits. Before the initial excitement inevitably wears off, their behaviour is often outrageously wanton. I'm forever gasping, groaning and guffawing at the scandalous misadventures recounted to me. Stop now if you don't want to read about vomiting, fist-fights, anal-sex and Viagra!

Reading through the pages of this book, you might cringe and think, 'this behaviour is appalling! These scumbags should be acting as ambassadors for their countries, not like depraved dipsomaniacs!' Indeed, plenty of seasoned ex-pats in Japan grumble that the kind of obnoxious escapades within these pages make all Westerners look bad.

Personally, I doubt the Japanese are narrow-minded enough to condemn all overseas visitors just because they saw me staggering down the high-street, drunk, with my trousers around my ankles, babbling incoherently. Most Japanese folk are good sports and, more often than not, are amused by the baffling buffoonery of crazy foreigners. Besides which, they get up to all manner of naughtiness themselves, from brazenly drooling over porno magazines in public, to necking beer at work gatherings until they spew. My friend recently witnessed a young Japanese guy strip entirely naked on a crowded commuter train, exuberantly shouting "I'm Japanese Jackass! Japanese Jackass!" which, for better or worse, is surely evidence of a growing international language of tomfoolery.

And so, this book is dedicated to the lovely people of Japan for being so much fun, and for putting up with the likes of me.

Messing with the Wrong Guy

A friend of mine once recounted a tale of woe that befell his colleague, a large and conspicuous Brit who had a reputation as a tough guy. Let's call him Dave. The big lad was sat alone in a bar in Kanagawa prefecture one night not long after his arrival in Japan, chatting to the barman about his first impressions of the country, when some other customers started to make him feel uncomfortable. Although the bar was lovingly decked out in American pop-cultural paraphenalia like neon Budweiser signs and framed pictures of Elvis Presley, it would seem that Westerners rarely set foot inside. A group of sun-tanned men in polyester suits were sat at a nearby table, and the smallest of their number kept gesturing in Dave's direction, muttering and sneering disdainfully. The few words Dave managed to pick up were nasty, (you always learn the rude words first,) and he got the nagging sensation these men weren't exactly keen on foreigners.

As Dave's unease mounted he started drinking with increasing velocity. He tried to ignore the pint-sized wise-guy and continue his conversation with the barman, but it became difficult when the unpleasant little character pointed in his direction and launched into a series of exaggerated baboon impersonations, scratching his head and making loud simian grunts and yelps, much to the amusement of his cronies. After a while this became too much for Dave to tolerate. He stormed over to the joker's table, picked up a brimming glass of beer and emptied it over the guy's curly-permed head, before punching him in his dripping, flabbergasted face. And with that, Dave strolled nonchalantly out of the bar.

Not the best course of action, I'm sure you'll agree. As a professional English teacher for a well-known franchise of language schools, you'd think he'd have sufficient linguistic skills to come up with a witty comeback. But, barely speaking Japanese, he was forced into action. Reduced to an inarticulate brute, he was unable to express himself but through violence- a bit like King Kong, which, in a way, vindicates his antagonist's ape-comparisons, I suppose.

Anyway, the next morning Dave was startled awake by the eardrum-shattering ring of his telephone. He remembered little of the evening before, but felt a vague sense of shame as he croakily answered the phone. He wasn't in the best state to receive the shocking news that was to follow.
The voice on the other end of the line told him to vacate his apartment immediately, he was in grave danger. It was a frantic Japanese colleague from his company speaking. Apparently the men he had clashed with the previous night were Yakuza- ruthless, scary gangsters with a huge, immensely powerful criminal network spreading across the country.
Oops.
Throughout the morning, groups of menacing men had been showing up at various branches of the chain of schools Dave worked for, asking for him by name and intimidating the staff. The barman Dave had been chatting to must have spilled the beans.

One can only imagine what horrors these goons had in store for Dave. Another acquaintance of mine, an amiable Texan named Justin, had once been chased down the street by a gang of Yakuza, wielding golf clubs, as punishment for the mere crime of speaking too loudly in a noodle bar, so who knows what wrath a punch in the face would inspire. These were men who cut off their own little fingers to save face.

Suffice to say, Dave was cacking his khakis. In a state of intense panic, he grabbed his wallet and passport, and fled. Soon after, the Yakuzas issued an invoice to Dave's company, demanding compensation for costs incurred while pursuing their employee, (travel expenses, petrol money, loss of earnings.) The school obligingly coughed up the cash without any argument, which goes to show the level of power these dangerous dudes have.

Meanwhile, no longer the hard man, Dave was holed up in a cheap Tokyo hotel, quivering with dread. Before the week was out he he had flown home to the UK. I hesitate to say this exile served him right for reacting like a violent yob, but it's surely a good advertisement for restraint.

Regurgitation

    After one too many beverages the previous evening, and about two hours of unsatisfying sleep, Kate valiantly hauled herself out of bed, threw some clothes on and left the house to go to the language school where she taught. These responsible actions were not motivated by a sense of professional duty, but driven by the fear that one more sick-day might get her fired.

Red-eyed, green-faced and reeking of stale lager, Kate staggered into a small booth to attempt to teach her first class. A trio of immaculate, pastel-coloured housewives awaited her at the round table within and greeted her in unison as she plopped herself into her revolving chair. When Kate began the lesson, her students were somewhat disconcerted at her dishevelled appearance and croaky voice, but they soon got into the swing of things, the role-plays about travel or shopping as always providing a diversion from their humdrum lives.

So far so good, thought Kate. But about ten minutes into to the lesson she suddenly felt a wave of nausea in her stomach and a surge of fluid in her throat. Oh no! Before she knew it she was spraying multi-coloured gunge all over the table and splashing the unsuspecting housewives like a diseased firehose.

Clutching their bile-soaked textbooks, the students sat agape, their puke-flecked faces quivering in horror as Kate spewed forth like Linda Blair in "The Exorcist."

After she had regained her senses, Kate apologised profusely to the traumatized students, who were remarkably sympathetic and forgiving under the circumstances. Suffice to say, this wasn't at all what they had been hoping for from that morning's lesson.

When later reprimanded by a cold-eyed manager, Kate blamed her rancid gushings on a case of food poisoning, caught from some sketchy Sukiyaki.

Something certainly came out of Kate's mouth that day that her students would never forget. "Repeat after me… Bleeeeeuuuuurgh!!!"

Half Pints

Trying to control a bunch of snot-nosed, sugar-crazed toddlers is challenging enough if you speak the same language as them, but if you don't, it's murder (especially when you've got a hangover.)

I once found myself reluctantly doing this kind of work in a small suburban town in the middle of nowhere, named Mitsukyo. In a brightly-lit, carpeted room, I had to sing and dance like Barney the purple bastard dinosaur, while children tried to punch me in the nuts and scrawl on my shirt with crayons. These feral youngsters were constantly fighting, biting and shrieking. Not a class went by without someone running out of the room in a flood of tears (usually me.) With hyperactive delinquents like this on the loose, acting like "The Children of the Corn," it's no wonder Japan's birth-rate is declining at such a rapid rate. One hour with these maniacal runts would be enough to make even the most tolerant man run screaming to the nearest vasectomy clinic.

Nevertheless, the parents seemed to think the sun shined out of their kids arses, and complained to the management if I ever uttered a cross word. These indulgent folk showered their little cherubs with gifts, dressed them up in Louis Vuitton and Burberry and patted them on their dyed-orange heads. The young mothers would peer affectionately through the window of the classroom as their little angels tried to batter my brains out with plastic baseball bats.

Japanese parents are so determined that their kids learn English, that they enroll them in language schools at ridiculously early ages, often when they're as young as two years old. These little tykes can't even speak Japanese, let alone master a foreign tongue. If this trend of educating increasingly young infants continues, they'll be paying teachers to speak English into pregnant women's bellies through ultrasound devices before long. Or have an English teacher present at the time of conception, stood by the bed, singing the ABC song while the couple are banging away.

It takes a certain talent to manage a class of demented midgets, a talent that I didn't have. Hopping like a kangaroo with my joints creaking, and wheezing "the wheels on the bus go round and round" was a monstrous challenge. I've heard of military detainment camps where US soldiers force prisoners of war to perform humiliating, degrading acts, or listen to repetitive kids' songs like the theme from "Sesame Street" over and over again, as a form of torture. Well this was essentially the same deal.

One sweltering summer's Saturday, frazzled after several hours of this stomach-ulcer inducing work, I was in serious need of a drink or several. Still clad in my shirt and tie, I limped out of the torture chamber of a school and into a nearby Western-style cocktail bar, just in time for the start of happy hour. I flopped onto a barstool and ordered a shot of whiskey to calm my shattered nerves. Ahhh.

A couple of hours later it was still light outside but I was pleasantly pickled, having worked my way through half of the cocktail menu. I was chatting idly to the convivial barman in my mangled Japanese when I noticed a flurry of activity outside the window. He explained that today was the day of Mitsukyo's annual summer festival.

Throughout the summer, each town and village in Japan has its own little celebration, and all the locals gather in traditional dress (delightful summer kimonos for the ladies and funny pyjama-type things for the blokes.) They drink sake, eat fried squid balls, and cheer as sweaty men in shorts carry portable shrines up the main shopping promenade. Never one to miss a party, and eager for a reminder why I was enduring such a dismal job, I drained my Singapore Sling and ventured outside to join the festivities.

I wandered onto a narrow, sloped shopping street packed with jovial people. There were strings of flags overhead and stands selling hot snacks and beer. A group of old geezers, already half-wasted and excited to see a foreigner attending their small-town festival, waved me over, handed me a paper cup of sake, and started asking me good-natured questions.

Noticing that I was overheated and sweating, my tie still suffocating me, the old blokes encouraged me to take my shirt off. I drunkenly complied and they slapped my pasty-white, exposed beer-belly amiably.

This kind of affable molestation of flabby male foreigners is commonplace in rural Japan.

At this point a cheer rose from the crowd as a beautifully crafted shrine appeared at the bottom of the street, held aloft by a group of chanting men wearing headbands. As I observed their slow progress up the street I was given a plastic cup of beer by the hospitable locals. I was rapidly getting drunker than Oliver Reed at a stag party. Much to the old fellas' amusement, I tied my necktie around my head, Rambo-style, in a comedy imitation of the shrine carriers.

By the time the shrine disappeared from view I was truly irrigated. Suddenly, at the bottom of the hill, I spotted something extraordinary and inconceivable. Walking towards me were a group of semi-naked women. I almost dismissed this as an alcohol and heatstroke-induced hallucination, but I rubbed my eyes and they were still there, as clear as daylight, Brazilian girls brazenly parading up the hill wearing nothing more than g-strings, glittering bras, and feather head-dresses. It would seem that the Mitsukyo festival had taken some inspiration from the Rio de Janeiro carnival. An insanely bravura move for a small summer festival in a titchy suburb. Mitsukyo town council clearly had lofty aspirations.

All the booze and humidity had got me hot and bothered already, but this latest spectacle had caused me to start foaming at the mouth. As the scantily clad divas drew closer, they started plucking giggling men from the crowd and dancing the samba with them. One particularily nubile beauty gestured in my direction, obviously recognising the potential entertainment-value of a giant, shirtless white man attempting Latin dancing. My elderly compadres, jeering excitably, shoved me in the girl's direction. Still clutching an overspilling beer in one hand, I found myself dancing lasciviously with the half-naked honey-skinned goddess, in front of a roaring audience. At this point I was so utterly hammered and over-excited that I lapped up the attention and started busting some killer dance moves, thrusting and grinding like an extra in a hip-hop video.

I was grinning at the crowd for approval when I suddenly noticed some small, familiar faces looking back at me. Oh no. I immediately became consumed with a sense of dread. There, witnessing the whole sordid scene, were a cluster of my infant students and their gobsmacked parents. They looked on, horrified, at their teacher, stripped to the waist and shitfaced, beer in hand, tie on head, humping a half-naked Brazilian woman's leg like an oversexed Bulldog. One mother frantically covered her child's confused eyes. My automatic, beer-addled reaction was to raise my glass in their direction, in a toast. Some beer slopped from my overfilled cup and hit the pavement before them with a splash.

This, I decided, would be a good time to hastily make my exit down a nearby alleyway.

Champagne in the Classroom

A friend of mine named Dan was the most popular teacher at the four-letter-named English school where he worked, and female students would hang around the school like groupies at an Elvis concert, hoping to catch a glimpse of him. All of this was rather inexplicable since he was an ordinary, skinny, twenty-five-year-old Australian. Consequently he relished the attention. The ladies, ranging from old biddies to housewives and schoolgirls, would come to his classes and swoon as he flirted and fluttered his eyelids, offering something akin to a low-rent escort service with a bit of English teaching thrown in. (No doubt, he provided some extra-curricular services too, if you know what I mean, but I won't go into that.)

And so, one day, when Dan announced that he was to quit the job and return to Australia, the students were devastated. It was like the Backstreet Boys announcing their break-up.

On his final day at work, the fans turned up in droves to bid Dan a tearful farewell. He had decided to leave in style by bringing a couple of bottles of champagne into the classroom.

The students cheered as he popped the cork out of the first bottle, foam spraying everywhere, (there were probably some subconscious Freudian phallic thoughts going on at that point,) and they gleefully accepted the paper cups of bubbly.

These small-town ladies had a low threshold for alcohol, and were soon flushed and giggling.

Attracted by the hysterical commotion, the top boss of the school sneaked down the hallway and snooped through the window of the classroom to see if there was anything untoward going on. This man liked to enforce the company policy of a sober, professional learning environment, and got ants in his pants if he saw a teacher so much as undo his top shirt button. Naturally he was incensed to witness a teacher getting smashed on the premises, plying old grannies and underage youths with booze. I suspect he was a teeny bit jealous, too.

The next morning, while eating toast in his box-like company apartment, Dan noticed a letter drop though the front door. It turned out to be a formal written warning from the English school, sternly advising him not to drink at work or fraternize with students ever again, or else he would be in grave trouble. This threat might have carried a little more weight, had it not been sent the day *after* he'd left the job. As it was, Dan wasn't exactly soiling himself with anxiety. He simply guffawed, and skipped into his bedroom to show the letter to the two students who were helping him pack his suitcases.

Arrival

Trevor's journey from the airport to his new home in the suburbs of Tokyo had been confused by countless obstacles and distractions: bright street-signs of indecipherable squiggles, ticket machines and traffic lights playing plinky plonky jingles. On the ram-packed train, a party of impossibly small school kids in matching yellow hats had giggled and goggled at the funny foreigner struggling with his suitcases. California-raisin-faced old ladies stared at him disapprovingly. He was startled by a train station toilet which greeted him in an electronic voice as he was unzipping his trousers.

When Trevor finally arrived at the vast concrete apartment building which was to be his new home, he was punch drunk from the sheer volume of foreign sights, sounds, and people he had tripped over and side-stepped on his epic voyage. After checking the A4 xeroxed map to confirm it was the right place, he knocked. There were grunts and shuffling sounds from inside, then the door was swung open by a very big, pasty-white man with a towel around his waist and a white beard of shaving foam. He glared at Trevor belligerently.

"Hi. I...er...think I live here. NOVA English Schools sent me"

"Oh fuck! They told me I'd have the place to myself

for at least a couple of weeks." The big guy boomed in an American accent. "The last guy only moved out yesterday!" He turned and stormed back into the apartment, leaving the newcomer standing at the doorstep.

After stepping tentatively inside, Trevor made a point of removing his shoes at the door. He'd heard this was customary, but muddy footprints in the hallway would indicate that the policy wasn't rigidly adhered to in this joint.

"Your room's the empty one on the right," yelled the large American from the bathroom.

The room was unfurnished but for a small cupboard and a cheap futon, still in it's cardboard box in the corner. As Trevor surveyed the room, the large man reappeared in jeans and a shirt, slapping aftershave on his throat.

"Er, listen man. I'm expecting company this evening so could you help me out and keep a low profile?"

"Oh.Yeah, actually I'll probably just hit the sack early. I'm drained after the flight."

"Usually I wouldn't ask. It's just that I figured I'd have the place to myself tonight."

"It's all right. I could do with a good night's sleep."

"Thanks dude." He slapped Trevor on the back and jogged out of the room, closing the door behind him.

Trevor unwrapped the futon, then began to unpack, taking out his clothes, CDs, "The Lonely Planet Guide." He was pinning up some posters when he heard the American guy talking on the phone in the hallway outside his room. "Oh shit! That sucks. Can't you just tell your boss to go screw himself? We got the place to ourselves for once, babe." He adopted a sulky, petulant tone. "What a pain in the ass. Yeah yeah, seeya."

After a brief silence there was a knock on Trevor's door. The American entered.

"I just realized I didn't introduce myself. I'm Paul," he offered his hand, and smiled.

"I'm Trevor. Nice to meet you."

"Listen, er...Trevor. I felt bad about ditching you on your first night, so I blew off my date. I thought I'd take you out and show you around the town," he said while looking appraisingly around the newly decorated room.

"Well, I'm a bit jet-lagged. I wouldn't mind an early night, if it's all the same to you."

"Come on! It's your first night in Japan. It's supposed to be a big night! We're new roomies, we should get to know each other. What do you say?" he exclaimed, shaking Trevor vigorously by the shoulders.

"Well all right, what the hell. Just give me a minute to get changed."

Trevor was perking up at the enthralling prospect of an night out in Tokyo.

"That's the spirit!" Paul hovered in the doorway. "Er. By the way, do you have any money on you? I forgot to go to the bank."

"Oh. Yeah, I've got a bit, but..."

"Great! Can you fix me up with a few bills until Wednesday? I get paid then."

"Yeah, I suppose so." Trevor fumbled hesitantly with his bundle of Japanese notes, the austere faces of unknown historical figures looking up at him while Paul looked on, eyes gleaming. "I don't know how much I've got here. I haven't figured out the exchange rate."

Paul snatched a couple of notes from from Trevor's hand and stuffed them in his pocket. "Thanks, bro! A couple of these bad boys should be just fine. I can already tell, me and you are gonna get along famously! Right, get your shit together, let's party!"

Trevor crossed the heaving dance floor with a bottle of beer in each hand, to the table where Paul was sat, smoking and scanning the room for available girls.

Paul had led the way to this lively bar through the bustling streets of Shinjuku, Trevor trailing, intoxicated by all the lights, noises, and colours of the neon nightlife district. What an incredible place, Trevor had thought. He'd seen all of this stuff in celluloid, in video games, and on the pages of manga comics. It was surreal to actually be there in reality.

"Cheers!" Trevor shouted over the music, raising his bottle of Kirin beer, and handing the other bottle to Paul.

"In Japan, it's "Kampai!" dude." Paul winked and knocked back his drink.

"Kampai!" Trevor toasted. "So, how long have you

been in Japan?"

"About eight months. I'm going home this Christmas," he said, distractedly. "I tell you, I'm going to miss the women the most." He leered over at two tan-skinned girls in hip-hop clothes, dancing.

"Yeah, I see what you mean! They're very pretty. So have you dated a Japanese girl, then?"

"What, are you fucking kidding? I can't get enough of them!"

"So, you've got a girlfriend?"

"I like to play the field, bro."

"I see."

Trevor looked over at a nearby table of drunken salaried workers, laughing raucously and downing drinks. This wild side of the Japanese was far from the image he'd had of them as buttoned-up workaholics. "It's funny. I thought the people would all be quite serious over here."

"Nope. They're always ready to party."

"Really?"

"Yeah. Hey, check this out." Paul leaned over to the next table, which was occupied by several sozzled men in suits, and one bored-looking young woman in a skirt-suit.

"This is my friend!" He exclaimed to them, while pointing at Trevor. "His first day in Japan!"

They nodded at Trevor. "Sugoi!"

"Where... do you from?" One man slurred, struggling to speak English.

"England." Trevor smiled. "I'm going to be an

English teacher. For NOVA"

"Ah, NOVA." They all said in unison, nodding in recognition. NOVA was an enormously successful chain of English conversation schools, as well-known and ubiquitous in Japan as McDonald's.

"Please teach me!" The English speaker quipped, and his pals all laughed. He poured some clear liquid into a small glass and handed it to Trevor. "Please try Japanese shochu. Very delicious!"

"OK!" Trevor raised his glass. "Kampai!"

After palming the newbie off onto the group of businessmen, Paul discreetly sidled over to the sole female member of the group, a delicately mesmeric, long-haired girl.

Trevor suspected this was Paul's sole motivation behind initiating the conversation with the group, since the American spent the rest of the evening chatting the girl up, and eventually disappeared with her though the front door. A remarkable feat, since he was so bloated and grizzled. Trevor doubted Paul enjoyed the same success in the States. While impressed that his room-mate had pulled such a stunning girl, Trevor was left with the difficult challenge of finding his way home.

The evening had turned out to be a hugely expensive all-night boozerama and at five AM, totally demolished and barely capable of walking, Trevor clumsily navigated his way back to the station. His errant room-mate had taught him how to use the ticket machine the previous night (you start by pressing the button which says "English") and had encouraged Trevor to always travel on a child's ticket, "because no-one ever checks and you can save half the money." Trevor did so, then, jet-lagged and pissed beyond comprehension, lurched onto the Yamanote line and immediately blacked out.

 When Trevor later awoke he was stupefied to discover he was still on the train. 'Where the hell am I?' he thought, looking around in panic. He was stupefied to discover the carriage was ram-packed with hundreds of businessmen and women, squashed in like sardines. It would seem Trevor had been dozing there for several hours, while the train endlessly circumnavigated the city, gathering passengers.
 He was stretched out over a whole row of seats and, although there were a multitude of people standing up on the train, crushing each others' balls and tits and gasping for air, nobody had dared disturb Trevor in order to get a seat. Perhaps this was because he had wet his pants at some point, and consequently he and the seats were dripping wet and stank of piss.
 A haggard wretch, blushing with shame, Trevor weakly pulled himself into a sitting position and tried to remember where he lived, while a hundred pairs of disquieting eyes glared silently at the grotesque beast in distaste. Welcome to Japan!

It's Curtains

A polite and well-mannered friend of mine named Robert was in a quaint little Japanese eaterie with some local pals, indulging in some native dishes and sipping sake. The exotic atmosphere of the traditional watering hole was a great source of pleasure for Robert, but after a while his legs grew numb from sitting on the hard tatami floor. He decided to stand up and stretch his legs for a while and, as he did so, he leaned against the wall. Unfortunately, it wasn't a wall, it was a curtain, and he plummeted through the drapes like a felled tree. Timbeeeeerrrrr!

There was an apocalyptic noise as Robert crash-landed onto a table in the adjoining room, sending plates of yakitori flying, and overturning cups of shochu.

A silence chilled the room as he feebly raised his rice-splattered body from the wreckage of the table, and brushed green beans and bits of fish from his clothes.

Seated around Robert were a group of sober-looking Japanese businessmen who moments earlier had been enjoying a civilized dinner after work, but were now paralyzed with shock, and dripping with miso soup.

The Hostess with the Mostess

One night, me and a handful of friends were in a poky late-night bar in Fujisawa city and got chatting to one of the regulars, a rotund, middle-aged man enigmatically wearing sunglasses. After a while, he told us that he wanted to move on to another joint, his favourite hostess bar, and he'd like us to join him. His treat.

Sozzled salarymen with low self-esteem regularly flock to hostess bars to enjoy the company of scantily-clad young ladies, who pour their drinks, light their smokes and laugh at their jokes. Being reduced to paying someone to talk to you may be considered suicidally depressing in the West, but in Japan it's a national past-time. We eagerly accepted (for the free drinks as much as anything.)

The guy excitedly led us down several dark, obscure back-alleys, until we arrived at a mysterious-looking place named "Safety." We approached cautiously, but the doormen greeted us enthusiastically, took our coats and welcomed us inside to a room full of boisterous laughter and revelry. There was a live band performing on a small stage, several tables of pissed-up businessmen and a number of attractive women in wigs, cocktail dresses and nurses' uniforms. This kind of bohemian abandon was distinctly un-Japanese, more akin to a 19th century French cabaret.

We were soon sat with shit-eating grins on our faces, guzzling whiskey and coke in the company of some amiable young ladies, apparently of South-East Asian extraction. We quickly got into the spirit of things, playing drinking games, singing karaoke and dancing.

These amorous women were very touchy-feely. One of them was sat next to me, stroking my knee suggestively with a lascivious smile on her face. I was certainly starting to see the appeal of hostess bars.

My enthusiasm quickly died, however, when she suddenly announced "I am a gay."

"Eh?" I said, nonplussed.

"I am a boy," she/he elaborated and it was only now that I noticed the croaky baritone of his/her voice. I slowly looked around me and it struck me- all the "girls" in the place had large hands and Adam's apples.

I turned, horrified, to the mysterious man who had brought us here. He removed his shades and smiled at me knowingly.

"Dear me, look at the time!" I stared at my watch theatrically. "We'd better be going," I exclaimed, flinging the manly hand from my upper thigh. Frantically, I gathered my friends and explained my discovery to them in a dissonant whisper, watching the blood drain from their faces as I did so. We made our excuses and escaped.

Unfortunately, in the heat of the moment, no-one stopped to tell my extremely wasted and gullible friend Ed, who was vomiting in the bathroom at the time. Come closing time, he gladly agreed to accompany the randy she-males back to their shared apartment. He soon realized his mistake, however, when he found himself being chased, naked and terrified, around the living room by several pre-op transsexuals. Yikes!

Inner Thoughts of a Jaded Eikaiwa Teacher

I sit on the half-empty train, engrossed in my book. The trees, mountains and perfectly manicured gardens now zooming past the window have long since lost their power to distract me.

I enjoy the peace and quiet of life out here in the countryside. The Japanese folk don't disturb me. Nobody talks to me, and I'm perfectly happy with this arrangement. I love being alone with my thoughts.

Suddenly, voices jolt me out of my daydeams. Further down the carriage sit two hulking foreigners in sportswear, conversing loudly in English. The presence of these two antisocial brutes makes me deeply uncomfortable. What the hell are they doing all the way out here, anyway? They must be from the military base. I hope they don't notice me or, Heaven forbid, want to talk to me. Please, God, don't let them see me!

The anxiety is making me sweat. I loosen my collar. One guy with a buzzcut and an open beer-can looks towards me and openly smiles, but I glance away, pretending not to have spotted him. Why should I be expected to interact with him just because he's another Westerner? I'll just ignore them and pray they go away.

I plug in my earphones and look down at my book, so I don't have to hear anyone, or make eye contact, for the rest of my journey.

Walking down the small high-street, I see the enormous sign looming over me, "NOVA," and I grimace. It's an eyesore, spoiling the quiet charm of this country town, (along with the 7/11 and the McDonald's.) However, it's also the only place that will sponsor my visa.

I'm in no mood for teaching today. It's a cruel irony that I moved out here to rural Japan for the solitude, and yet I'm paid to talk to people. I hate having to smile and affect cheerfulness all day.

I unplug the earphones from my ears as I mount the stairs. Ayako, the receptionist, smiles at me as I enter, which makes my first moments at work bearable.

"Ohayo!" She chirps, by way of greeting. "Genki?"

"Genki!" I reply, which I means I'm fine, although I actually feel like death. "Genki?"

"Genki desu!" I don't know how she manages maintain this level of enthusiasm all day. Must be the Japanese diet. She really is quite delightful, though. I must find out if she's single.

I enter the teachers' room and I'm displeased to see that the manager, Jen, has already arrived, and is sitting, doing paperwork. She's wearing a pin-striped suit and spectacles, and her hair is pinned back. She nods at me curtly and I reciprocate, before stepping, with mounting dread, towards the paper schedule that is pinned to the wall each morning. I breathe a sigh of relief when I see that I will be teaching no children today. "Thank god for that!" I rejoice, and Jen responds with a raised eyebrow. She takes her job extremely seriously. I pull the file of my first student out of the cabinet, sit down and flick disconsolately through a nearby textbook, trying to find a suitable lesson. They all seem rubbish to me but I haven't the energy or motivation to think of something new right now. I pick a lesson at random, already suspecting the class will be a pointless waste of both mine and the student's time. Then the god-forsaken bell rings for the start of my first class. The death knell.

Elderly Japanese gentlemen exude a certain dignity and politeness that I admire. My first student, Mr Goto, is one such man. But although he's pleasant, he's incredibly boring and has shocking dentistry and breath.
He smiles as I enter. Jesus, his teeth are horrible. They're long, like fangs, and stained beige by nicotine and green-tea. The way they jut out of his mouth almost looks like he's playing pan-pipes.
"Good morning, Mr. Ian!" He stands and bows as I enter the room. He is wearing a neat, three-piece suit. Mr Goto is always well-groomed, so it's all the more astonishing to me how brazenly he dismisses oral hygiene.
I shiver as I catch a glimpse of his graveyard of a

mouth, teeth jutting out like filthy, neglected headstones, then I regain my composure, and turn on the mock-enthusiasm. "Good morning, Mr Goto! Please, sit down. And how are you today?"

"Fine, thank you, and you?"

"Pretty good. How was your weekend?"

"Marvellous. Yesterday I went to hot spring with my wife, my daughter and my son-in-law."

"Really? How was it?" I enquire mechanically. I'm operating on automatic-pilot now, having been through this routine countless times times before.

"It was wonderful. And after hot spring, we had a lunch. Sushi. It was very delicious."

"That sounds good! I love sushi." In reality, I haven't eaten sushi in months. I always go to McDonald's for lunch, and hate myself for it. Anyway, I can't think about food now, when Mr Goto's teeth look like the ribcage of a rotting rat-carcass sticking out of his mouth.

"The weather is nice today, isn't it?" He grins.

"Yes, it's a beautiful day." His breath stinks like a cat's anus, and makes me recoil. I remember the scene in the film "The Silence of the Lambs," when the forensic examiner performing an autopsy on a dead body smears menthol on his top lip to block out the hideous stench, and I consider the possibility of adopting the same technique the next time I teach Mr Goto. "Anyway, let's get on with today's lesson. I thought today we'd practice conditionals. So please open your book to page thirty seven."

Now it's over to the textbook, and I'm in fully-automatic mode. As I steer the student through the lesson, I make a mental shopping list. Must remember to buy milk and bread on the way home from work. And some digestive biscuits to have with my coffee.

Later, when I enter the classroom for my next lesson, I'm much more buoyant, for awaiting me is a sweetly pretty young stewardess named Hiromi, sitting upright and beaming. That's more like it! Girls like that don't give me the time of day back home, but Hiromi hangs on my every word. Now I remember why I stick with this job. I can't believe I get paid for this.
But, tragically, sat next to her is Atsuko, a pig-ugly old hag with the dopey demeanour of a retired bare-knuckle boxer who's had too many blows to the cranium. This woman has the memory span of the guy in "Memento." She instantly forgets everything I teach her.
"What's the date today, Atsuko?"
"Uh...April twenty tooth."
"You mean 'second'"
"April second tooth"
Oh God. This woman always sucks the life out of me. She's an energy vampire. She comes in, drains all of the enthusiasm and vitality out of me like I'm some kind of spiritual petrol pump, then she leaves, feeling refreshed and invigorated. She's like a "Dementor" from the Harry Potter books, she sucks all the joy and cheerfulness out of the room.

Why do these people want to learn English? Why do people come here? I just can't understand it. And most of all, I really resent that that my income, my visa, my company apartment, and my whole way of life is entirely dependent on them. As the students converse in broken English, I slump lethargically in my chair, with a forced smile and an occasional nod.

Gaijin Ghetto

I used to share a flat, high up on the seventh floor of a vast, concrete apartment building in Fujisawa city. Returning home late one night, a little tipsy and gormlessly munching on a 7/11 hot dog, I squeezed into the tiny elevator and nudged the button for my floor.

I strode the two paces from the elevator to my front door, which was unlocked – evidently my room-mates were already home, no doubt playing video games or watching a DVD. I prized my shoes off and navigated my way down the unlit corridor and into the living room.

When I entered the room I was surprised to see a Japanese family sat on the floor around a short-legged kotatsu table. A mother and her young daughter and son sat sedate under the colourful glow of an inane variety programme on the television.

"What the...?" I mumbled, my beer-befuddled brain struggling to find an explanation for the presence of these intruders, who were now staring back at me in a disquieting way. 'Why the hell have a Japanese family set up camp in my house?' I pondered to myself as I gazed at them with a furrowed brow.

The three of them looked petrified, faces contorted in a silent scream of horror, like that Munch painting multiplied by three (or maybe multiplied by six, since

I was drunk.)

It gradually dawned on me that I was in the wrong flat. The family looked up in justifiable dread at the giant foreign monster who had invaded their harmonious home.

Mouth full of half-chewed hot-dog, I blurted an apology and ske-daddled out of there.

It would seem that I had pressed "six" rather than "seven" in the elevator.

This kind of occurrence was commonplace in the building, known among local ex-pats as as the "Gaijin Ghetto" due to the high volume of foreign tenants within. (The term "gaijin", as you probably know, means "foreigner" in Japanese. It's considered a derogatory term by some but, when describing some of the mischievous misfits in these stories, derogatory terms seem more than reasonable.) I feel sorry for the Japanese residents in the building, who had to put up with the pumping music late at night, the animal-house tomfoolery, blatant disregard for local customs, and frustrating encounters in broken Japanese.

The Gaijin Ghetto housed an incestuous little community, with lots of love affairs, gossip, in-fighting, back-stabbing, betrayal and sex. Sort of like an expatriate Melrose Place. One couple residing there were Ian and Sophie, both of whom were friends of mine. The pair of them were nice individually, and perfectly pleasant while sober, but if you introduced alcohol into the equation, they would invariably end up having huge, violent, earth-shattering arguments with each other. They were both prone to massive shouting fits and tantrums, and any all-night karaoke jam to which they were invited would result in much broken glass, tears and strained vocal chords. I did my best to remain neutral on such occasions.

Late one night I was happily dozing on my futon, when I was abruptly awoken by my mobile-phone ringing. Before I answered the call I saw Sophie's name flashing on the screen, and groaned. Another hellish row must have taken place. These 3AM calls were a fairly regular occurrence. When I answered, I could hear her sobbing. It transpired that she and Ian had just had another epic screamathon, and she had stormed out of the apartment, weeping.
"Can I come up and stay at your place tonight?" Sophie whimpered. "Me and Ian have broken up. This time it's for good."
I'd heard this story several times before, so I was sceptical. I was also feeling way too tired to be the shoulder to cry on yet again, like some kind of asexual sidekick from a romantic comedy.
"Oh, all right, but you'll have to stay on the sofa." I grumbled, wary of letting her stay in my room, for fear of my roommates' suspicions fueling yet more gossip in the Gaijin Ghetto. "But I'm in bed, so let yourself into the flat. The door's unlocked. I've got to sleep. I'm working early tomorrow."
And with that I hung up and went back to sleep.

The following morning I wandered into the living room, yawning and scratching my arse. Sophie was

47

nowhere to be seen, so I assumed she had already been and gone. This theory proved to be wrong, however, when minutes later she burst through the front door, breathless and hysterical. I made some coffee and listened to her story.

The night before, not wanting to awaken me or my roommates, Sophie had crept into the apartment without switching the light on, then tip-toed down the hallway and into the living room. Unable to find the sofa in the darkened room, she curled up on the floor and drifted into a deep sleep.

In the morning, she woke up in a heap, hair messed-up and mascara smeared all over her face like Robert Smith from The Cure, her joints aching from a night spent on the hard floor. As her eyes slowly adjusted to the bright sunlight, she was startled to see a small, bewildered boy staring at her with a mixture of curiosity and fear.

Her head darted around, and she realized that she was in an unfamiliar room. There was a small shrine in one corner, and framed Japanese calligraphy and school photos were mounted on the walls. It would seem, in her drunken and emotional state, she had entered and slept all night in the wrong apartment.

She suddenly heard adult voices speaking in Japanese from within another room and frantically she leaped to her feet and scrambled past the boy, down the hallway and out of the front door.

As coincidence would have it, it turned out to be the very same apartment that I had previously stumbled into. I suspect the poor souls have started locking the door.

Up All Night

Mike was an instructor for a massive language school corporation, where he served up insubstantial lessons like pimply teenagers dish out chicken nuggets, and accordingly he didn't take his job too seriously. And so it was, that one Monday morning the young Brit was still phenomenally drunk from the previous weekend and not feeling well at all. He was on his knees, dry-heaving and drooling into the toilet bowl, when he heard his American room-mate, Aaron, in the doorway behind him, and looked over his shoulder.

Aaron was suited and booted for work, and smirking. "Heavy night, huh? Jesus, look at you, man. Are you going to work like that?"

Mike nodded, wondering how on Earth he was going to make it through the day.

"You gonna call in sick?"

It hadn't occurred to Mike that he was one short phone call away from a day in bed. A very attractive proposition indeed. Despite some outrageous drinking sessions during his three months in Japan, Mike had yet to take a day off work. "I dunno. What do you think?"

"Why not? I do it all the time. They don't pay you for sick days anyways, so they're not losing out. It won't make you too popular with the manager, though."

Mike stared down at his bloodshot eyes reflected in

the toilet water. What kind of an impression would he make if he showed up for work in this condition, anyway?

"If you're sick you have to phone the head office, so they can find someone else to fill in for you." Aaron pulled out his mobile phone. "Leave it to me. I'll just pretend I'm you. They'll never know the difference." After a pause, Aaron spoke in an appallingly fake British accent, like Dick Van Dyke in 'Mary Poppins.' "Well, 'ello there. Is that the foreign personnel department?... I don't think I can make it in to work today. I really am frightfully sorry!" He winked at Mike. "My name? It's Mike... My family name? Sure, it's..." He covered the handset.

"Benson!" Mike whispered frantically.

Aaron uncovered. "It's Benson... B. E. Double N. S. O. N"

"One N!!"

"Sorry, I mean one N."

Mike looked on helplessly at this car crash of a phone call.

"Which branch do I work at? Well, let's see, now what's it called again?"

"Machida!" Mike spat.

"I think its called Machida. Yes, that's it... What's my problem? Well..." He grinned at Mike. "It's quite embarrassing. The thing is, I think someone slipped some Viagra in my drink last night because I've...well... I've got a huge erection that I can't get rid of."

Mike looked on, transfixed with horror. Aaron was struggling not to laugh. "It's really difficult to hide. You can see it sticking out quite prominently. I just don't think it would be appropriate for me to come to work. I hope I haven't let everyone down. Could you apologize to my co-workers and explain the problem for me? I do so hate to disappoint people. Cheerio mate!"

He hung up and roared with laughter. Mike stared in disbelief at his room-mate for a moment, then turned and puked into the toilet once more.

Private Lessons

One of Japan's best known English schools forbids its instructors from meeting their students outside of the classroom. Randy teachers, hoping to get lucky with the hot office ladies and nurses in their charge, whine about this despotic cock-blocking. Their sense of injustice is especially strong after hearing accounts from crusty old colleagues about the good old days before the loathed policy was introduced. Apparently the school was a veritable pick-up joint. Teachers were collecting phone numbers in class and getting furtive blow jobs under the desks. Particularly during the bohemian "bubble economy" years of the eighties and nineties, each day at work was akin to a Roman orgy.

The company chiefs claim the "non-fraternization policy" is in place solely to protect the teachers, but I suspect the real motive is to stop their customers from getting any "free English" from the teachers outside of working hours. In this respect, the company is much like a pimp, and the teachers are its "ho"s. If the customers want the goods, they have to give the pimp a slice of of the action.

This ban is controversial because whether or not it can be legally enforced is something of a grey area. Indeed, one disgruntled employee, fired for dating a student, successfully sued the school for unfair dismissal.

Nonetheless, teachers who date their students rarely risk mentioning their extra-curricular antics at work, for fear of getting into trouble. Meanwhile, their bosses tend to avoid the topic, so as not to get mixed up in any complicated legal issues. It's not unlike the "don't ask, don't tell" arrangement for gay people in the US military.

Anyway, all of this is immaterial because most of the employees of said language-school are mutinous malcontents who wouldn't let a little rule stop them from having fun. In fact, the policy introduces elements of mystique and danger to any student-teacher fling, which serve to make things even more sexy and exciting for those involved.

Below are a handful of cases of teachers breaking the much-maligned rule. These incidents are most definitely just the tip of the iceberg.

Brent, an instructor in an eikaiwa, was secretly dating one of his pupils, a nubile university student named Kaori. After romance blossomed over the textbooks, they had exchanged telephone numbers and, later, bodily fluids. They had taken their relationship from the classroom to the bedroom, moving from one type of intercourse to another, so to speak. Things were progressing well, or so Brent thought, until one fateful day.

Brent was sitting in the staff room, quietly eating some sushi for lunch, when he heard a commotion from the front desk, down the hall. A furious middle-aged woman had charged into the building and was ranting in Japanese to the managerial staff. Brent would later discover that this was none other than Kaori's mother, fuming about her daughter's affair with Brent. "Do you know what that *animal* did to my poor, innocent daughter?!"

It would seem Kaori, in a moment of guilt, had taken it upon herself to share with her mother every sordid detail of her bedroom dealings, and the old lady hadn't liked what she'd heard one bit. Now, at considerable volume, the enraged mother was passing the information on to Brent's superiors. The Japanese staff were frantically trying to pacify her, before all the other customers could hear her shrieking about cunnilingus, buttock fondling and heavy petting.

Later that day, Brent was called into his manager's office to be interrogated about his student-shagging. He denied everything. "I have no idea what you're talking about," Brent protested. Sadly for him, Kaori's resourceful mum had cajoled her daughter into drawing a detailed map of the interior of Brent's apartment as proof that she'd been there. This evidence was considered sufficiently damning by Brent's boss to warrant dismissal.

Fired and stunned, Brent trudged home to pack his bags.

Alex felt odd entering the classroom, for he was about to teach a lesson to a girl he'd slept with the very night before. There were two other students booked into the class, so he would have to put on his teacher face, and spout patronizing comments and platitudes throughout the lesson. It would be awkward correcting the girl's grammar mistakes, when less than twenty four hours ago, the two of them had been making the beast with two backs on his sweat-drenched single futon. But then again, the secret knowledge of this forbidden rendezvous would certainly make the lesson more scintillating. Perhaps they could exchange knowing winks, or play footsie under the table.

In the classroom, behind the kidney-bean-shaped desk, the aforementioned young lady was perched between a retired civil-servant and another girl: an attractive kindergarten teacher.

Alex liked to warm up his classes with a little banal banter, so he asked the old man what he had done the previous night.

"I went to Italian restaurant with my wife."

"Really? That's nice. Although, you should say 'an Italian restaurant.' How about you, Hiromi?" With a sly raised eyebrow, he cheekily directed the same question at the girl he had bedded, and wondered how she would rise to the challenge. "What did you do last night?"

"I fucked you," she stated, matter-of-factly.

Gulp. Clearly this girl was not one to mince with

words. Alex hadn't expected her to actually tell the truth. This outburst could spell serious trouble if the boss ever found out. Alex gritted his teeth, and his face turned crimson. "Oh...I...er.." Attempting to maintain a veneer of professionalism, he swiftly turned to the kindergarten teacher and, stammering slightly, asked her the same inane question. "So,...Yuko...what did you g-get up to last night?"

This time, the inquiry was greeted with silence. Yuko was staring hatefully at Alex, and her cheeks were burning a shade of red to rival Alex's own. You see, I neglected to mention before that Alex had slept with her, too, a few weeks before. She had been hoping to take the relationship to another level, so it was maddening to hear news of his sleazy parlour games from a loose-lipped love-rival. Yuko only refrained from screaming herself hoarse because there was a respectable old gent sat in the room, unaware he was in the midst of a deadly love triangle.

Alex had been an undercover Lothario for quite some time, treating the classroom like a meat/black-market. He had taken advantage of the school's "no-socializing" policy to the fullest. The cloak of secrecy had allowed the nefarious love-rat to conduct several illicit affairs at the same time, without being busted...until now!

After the deeply uncomfortable forty-minute class was finally over and Alex had escaped to the staff-room, the two women got talking. They soon learned all about his dastardly two-timing. They, in turn, told several other students with whom they were friendly, and it quickly transpired that naughty Alex had been getting jiggy with a fair few of their number.

Word travels fast among gossiping eikaiwa students. The jig was up. Before long, a group of six women were gathered in front of the school, bickering with each other, squabbling about who had staked claims on Alex first, who he liked most, and who was in the wrong. Eventually, united by their fury at Alex, they put their differences aside and focussed on a common goal. Like a witches coven, they plotted revenge. Hell hath no fury like several women scorned.

The six splenetic ladies marched into the reception area of the language school and demanded to see the manager. Alex's boss was dumbstruck as the gang of irate women strode into his poky little office and, one after another, began to regale him with tales of Alex's despicable deceptions and debauchery.

As the manager sat, gob-smacked, listening to these astonishing horror stories, he reached for the drawer containing the dismissal papers.

Alex hadn't so much broken the rules, as pissed all over them from a very great height!

Of course, it's not only the teachers who gleefully exploit the covertness that the anti-fraternization policy creates. A friend of mine named Tim was scandalized when a glamourous student he had been surreptitiously dating for several months revealed over dinner in a sushi restaurant that they would have to break up because she was to be married to another.

"What? Married? Who to?!" Tim choked on his rice.

"To my boyfriend."

"'Boyfriend?' I though *I* was your boyfriend."

"He's Japanese. We have to get married because I'm pregnant." She explained.

"P...p...pregnant?!" Tim was lost for words upon hearing this second bombshell. Not only had his girlfriend been cheating on him, she was also expecting a baby.

After the girl reassured him that he was not the father, the crestfallen cuckold wandered out of the restaurant and into a dimly-lit local bar, to drown his sorrows with hard liquor.

Later that night, James, a fellow teacher from Tim's school, entered his favourite bar and was surprised to see his colleague slumped, cheerlessly, over the bar.

"Hi Tim! Why the long face?" James enquired.

Tim looked up from his whiskey. "My girlfriend has just dumped me," he blubbed. "She's getting married to someone else. And she's p...pregnant."

James looked as if he'd seen a ghost. "Wait as second, what's her name?"

"Chisako. She's one of our students, if you must know. Short, black hair. Works for Panasonic."

James shook his head, stunned. "I don't believe this. I just heard the same story from her yesterday! I've been dating Chisako for six months!"

The despondent duo were silent for a moment. While

this latest revelation slowly soaked into Tim's mashed mind, James ordered two large shots of whisky.

Moronic Motorcycle Madness

 One late summer's night, as me and some friends spilled drunkenly out of a karaoke club, we encountered a bleached-blonde teenager, sat astride his motorbike in the neon-lit street. He was obviously a member of the pesky motorcycle gangs who keep everyone in Tokyo awake at night, revving their engines and honking the theme from "The Godfather" on their horns. These youngsters, called the "Bosozoku", scare the hell out of elderly Japanese folk, but are usually nice to foreigners, perhaps feeling a kinship in the shared outsider status.
 A member of our party realized that the kid was a pupil at the local public high school where he taught English. We struck up an amiable chat with the lad about his bike, and he excitedly offered to take one of the girls, a petite blonde named Natasha, for a spin around the block on his prized possession. She hopped on the back and they sped around the corner at high speed. The engine was roaring, and Natasha clutched the youngster for dear life. When they reappeared a few minutes later at the opposite end of the narrow street, the kid was beaming, and we all clapped and cheered as Natasha bounced off the motorbike.

 Being prone to moronic behaviour while sloshed, and seeking a cheap thrill, I said "me next!" and flopped onto the back of the high-schooler's bike, weighing the thing down dramatically. He looked a bit wary- it was a small contraption and I'm a big bloke. The thing was buckling under my immense weight. Even so, throwing caution to the wind, the teenager shrugged, took off at lightning speed, and we zoomed down the street.

This was a disaster waiting to happen. As the bike started wobbling under the strain of my beer-bloated frame, I started to worry about not wearing a crash helmet and suddenly remembered that I'm a pathetic coward. "OK, you can stop now. Just let me off here please. Ha ha!" I whimpered. The adrenaline-freak teen didn't understand this, however, and took it as a request to speed up. We were soon soaring along like StreetHawk, me crapping my pants and crying frantically "Slow down! Stop, you maniac! Let me off! I want to get off, you bastard!!" Suddenly, with an epic "wham!" the bike fell on its side and we were skidding on the tarmac. There was a screech of metal scraping against the ground, and sparks flying everywhere. Bam! We hit a metal dustbin at full force, like in a scene from a 70s movie. One of my trouser-legs was ripped to shreds and a sleeve of my shirt had been torn clean off. Looking like a jaded Incredible Hulk, I staggered to my feet and helped the dazed youngster up. He had blood gushing from his mouth but was laughing like a madman, the experience evidently having been a huge rush.

His expression soon changed, however, when he spotted his mangled bike lying in pieces behind him. The dents and scratched paintwork were of far more concern to him than his bleeding face, and he started forlornly trying to put the crumpled mess back together, as my stunned friends ran towards us to help. Simply happy to have survived the idiotic accident without breaking any bones, I eventually wandered home to bed. My complacency proved to be a tad premature. When I woke up the next morning in agonising pain, I soon discovered that large sections of my skin had been ripped off along with my clothes. I've still got scars from that little escapade. I looked down at my bruises and scratches that morning, and groaned as the events of the previous night emerged through the fog of my vast hangover. What a wanker I am!

The bedsheets were caked in dried blood. Remembering the biker gangs' "Godfather" horns, I half expected to find a severed racehorse's head in the bed. Unpleasantly, one sheet was stuck to the bloody wound on my arm. Wincing at the intense sting, I had to slowly peel it off, reopening the congealed gash with a sound like Velcro being pulled apart. Not the best way to start the day, I'm sure you'll agree- I would have preferred breakfast in bed.

Despite my pain, I couldn't help but feel more sorry for the teenager whose bike had been trashed. It must be a terrible blow to have your pride and joy reduced to wreckage. But at least, as a teacher, I take some comfort in the knowledge that I taught him a valuable lesson that night: Never, ever, offer rides to inebriated, fat foreigners.

Mayhem at the Massage Parlour

A booze-sponge at the best of times, my friend Pat was particularly smashed one winter's night, while reeling his way through Yokohama on his own after a welcoming party in his honour. He found himself cornered by two smiling ladies, who linked arms with him.

One post-pub obstacle for the drunken gaijin male navigating his way home, is the "massage" girl. These Chinese or Korean women lurk in dark doorways at night, hoping to persuade shit-faced businessmen to part with their wages in return for a massage, with a happy ending, followed by an unhappy epilogue when the money changes hands. Relying on the moral laxity of wasted blokes to make their living, these ladies pursue any man who is alone and drunk, with their trademark cry "Massaji? Massaji?" You can easily spot them because, in contrast to local Japanese girls who wear make-up, short-skirts and high-heels, the massage-ladies wear jeans and ski-jackets. (Yes, everything in Japan is up-side-down.)

A naïve newbie, Pat hadn't encountered these kind of women before, and was soon being led down a darkened staircase. The guileless bastard didn't know where they were taking him, but he was so moonstruck by the booze, he didn't care. He was pleased by this mysterious turn of events.

Inside the building he was dragged through a waiting room with a tiger-skin rug. A furtive man with a goatee sat behind a desk, smoking and watching the news on a portable television. The two girls took Pat through to a wide, sterile room full of the turquoise plastic curtains usually seen surrounding hospital beds. He was led behind one set of curtains where, sure enough, a flimsy single bed on wheels was waiting, on which he was invited to sit.

Pat sat there gormlessly as one girl disappeared and the other offered him refreshment in the form of a tumbler of brown liquid. She eagerly shoved the tumbler into Pat's gob and poured it down his gullet. He spluttered as he gulped down this potent concoction- apparently oolong tea spiked with a shit-load of whiskey. Presumably this bit of hospitality was a routine trick, to make the clientelle drunk and thus more loose with their cash, but it was rather unnecessary in this particular case, since Pat was already utterly mashed. More fire-water was the last thing he needed.

Pat surveyed the blurred girl credulously as she helped herself to a few notes from his wallet. She then began to undress him, as if he were a slow child. He was soon clad only in boxer-shorts and lying face-down, bewildered, on the hospital bed, receiving a brutal back massage. The girl was walking on his back, while hanging from bars attached to the ceiling, like a sordid gymnast. Pat's back went "snap, crackle" and "pop" like a bowl of Rice Krispies.

His dopey mush was squashed against a hole in the bed, custom-made to allow the customer to breathe while lying on his front. Suddenly, the sledge-hammer impact of the horrible brown potion he had drunk hit him with full force, and before he knew it Pat was puking though the hole, spraying pints of rancid booze all over the floor. He heard a shriek, the weight on his back was lifted, the curtain fluttered.

After a while, he woozily pulled himself up and discovered that the girl had gone. The movement of sitting up made him heave once more and he spewed another litre of brown nastiness onto the bedsheets and curtains.

Pat sat there on the puke-soaked bed for quite some time, feeling fuddled. He had come to Japan for the cherry blossoms and ancient temples, not to throw up on himself in a massage-parlour.

The girl didn't return. Eventually Pat began to get impatient, frustrated that he had been tricked out of a large wedge of cash. He resolved to restore some pride by getting his money back. He stormed through the curtains, single minded in purpose.

Pat raged through the building with the ruthless determination of the Terminator looking for Sarah Connor… if the Terminator had been wearing only his underpants and covered in sick.

Pat began ripping open the green curtains, and was greeted by the repulsive sight of the wrinkly flesh of middle-aged businessmen getting tug-jobs. These sleazy old geezers were utterly petrified to to see a towering, half-naked gaijin interrupting their horseplay (a furious boyfriend perhaps?) and shrieked for mercy.

The snarling, vomit-drenched buffoon burst through an unmarked door and into a room full of girls in ski-jackets nonchalantly playing cards. Surprisingly, they didn't seem particularly startled by the intrusion, and looked on calmly as the underpant-clad maniac ranted about how they had ripped him off. Pat demanded his cash back instantly, but the language barriers meant they hadn't a clue what he was shouting about.

He sighed. Time for plan B. By now fully aware of the nature of the pervy operation he was patronizing, Pat reasoned that if he wasn't getting his money back, he might as well get what he had paid for. With his hands, he gestured towards his groin pathetically, with a pleading look on his face. The looks of bemusement on the girls' faces told him no sex would be forthcoming. Standing in front of an entire room of prostitutes, wearing only undies, and begging for sex, was a new low for Pat.

Defeated, he bowed his head in shame and wearily blundered back to his curtained room to gather his clothes, praying that he would forget this unsavoury incident in the morning.

Late one night, not long after hearing Pat's sorry story, I was staggering home when I found myself the target of one particularly old and wrinkly "massaji" lady with kimchee-breath. As she pursued me down the street, I remembered Pat's misfortune and gained pace, being less than keen to get involved, despite her borderline-criminal groping. She was so persistant that I actually had to run to escape her foul clutches. I drunkenly ran straight into a concrete wall, chipped a front tooth and got a lump on my forehead the size of a golf-ball. But at least I still had my pride, which is more than can said for poor old Pat.

Attention, Class

I should take a moment here to apologize for the paucity of stories involving female teachers. I wish I had some juicy tales to divulge about the naughty sins of western women in Japan, but I can't think of anything except for a Canadian girl who went home with a different US serviceman every night. Ho-hum.

In fact, contrary to the experiences of western men, who blissfully wander the streets of Tokyo having their egos massaged and feeling ten feet tall, western women often have a tough time in Japan, and don't always get to enjoy the same care-free abandon as the guys. As well as having to deal with out-dated views on equality, they are often subjected to the unwanted advances of drunken businessmen while on their way home at night. Added to that are irksome encounters with a nightmarish selection of perverts with wandering hands on overcrowded trains, fiendish flashers and peeping Tomohiros.

I've heard many a spine-chilling tale from female friends- like the girl who arrived home from work to find a golden plaque had been anonymously stuck to her front door, on which was engraved, "I love your purple panties." She had been wearing said garment the previous night, and must have neglected to close the curtains. Creepy!

One poor lass even got flashed at by a man who was

masturbating while riding a bicycle. Quite a party trick, but not a pleasant spectacle when you're walking alone down a dark alleyway.

Meanwhile, foreign guys are generally oblivious to these sinister goings-on, believing the Japanese to be capable of nothing more nasty than littering. But there are, of course, occasions when men, too, find themselves the victims of unwanted attention.

My friend Ethan arrived home at his poky second-floor apartment one evening, exhausted after several hours of teaching. After he unlocked the door, kicked off his shoes and staggered into the living room, much to his surprise he discovered one of his students, a nurse, waiting for him on the sofa. A major shock to the system after a mundane day in an English conversation school.

The obsessive woman had been pursuing Ethan for quite a while, booking lessons with him as often as possible, and persistently hanging around outside the school. Finally, she had somehow got hold of his address and broken into his flat after climbing onto his balcony. This was an audacious invasion of privacy, behaviour which could be legitimately branded as stalking.

Thoughts raced through Ethan's mind when he laid eyes on the crazy woman, sat there smiling at him suggestively. What should he do? Throw her out into the street or try to talk to her? Notify his superiors at work, or call the police and seek a restraining order?

His decision? He shagged her.

Now it's fair to say that this was an unorthodox course of action, and surely not one that experts would recommend. However, it seemed to do the trick. She never bothered him again. Far from disturbed by the experience, the one thing which bothered Ethan was the girl's loss of interest after he'd delivered the goods. He took this as something of a slight on his performance.

Confused? Well, don't look at me, this ain't a psychology book.

Sizzling Sick

After an afternoon of indulgence in a Tokyo bar, me and two friends decided it was time for some grub, and hungering for some tasty local delicacies, we found ourselves in an okonomiyaki restaurant. My pal Max, the worse for wear after innumerable pints of Guinness, sat pinned in the corner of the booth next to his girlfriend Laura.

For those who don't know, okonomiyaki is like a pancake full of meat, seafood and vegetables, which customers cook, themselves, on a hotplate at the table. "Okonomiyaki" is also used as a slang term for the puddles of puke that litter train station platforms on a Friday night, courtesy of shit-faced businessmen after overzealous drinking parties. Regardless of this comparison, it's a very scrummy dish.

In the restaurant we soon received our orders and, feeling ravenous, I drunkenly set about cooking my nosh. I licked my lips as I clumsily spread the gooey ingredients over the sizzling hotplate, trying not to sear my flesh in the process.

It was then that I noticed Max's pained expression and greasy white face, like a pale slab of clay. Evidently all the booze he'd drunk, combined with the aroma of frying squid, was too much for him. Sat on the inside of the booth, he started struggling frantically to get past Laura. It was too late. With a look of wild panic in his eyes, his cheeks inflated like Louie Armstrong and I knew we were in for trouble. In slow-motion, a jet of black Guinness-puke sprayed from his uncomprehending face and hit the red hot metal before us with an almighty splash. The lumpy effluent sizzled and bubbled on the hotplate as we all looked on, stunned to silence. Immediately the room was filled with the foul stench of barbecued vomit.

My eyes were watering from the hideous stink and I began to retch. Customers at other tables were glaring in our direction.

"Check please!"

Japanese Justice

The Japanese police are a tolerant bunch compared to their Western counterparts- I once witnessed a cop being punched in the face by a drunken teenager and, while the youngster could expect a swift bullet through the face for doing such a thing in the US of A, the J-cop simply sent him on his merry way with a few stern words, evidently attributing the incident to youthful high spirits. Boys will be boys!

The same leniency, however, is not always extended to foreigners. I once met an enormous Aussie man-mountain named Matt, who told me about an unfortunate run-in he'd had with the police.

One night, after an enjoyable suburban pub crawl, Matt realized he'd lost his wallet somewhere along the way, so he decided to retrace his steps to look for it. Tenaciously, he searched the darkened streets, returned to each and every bar he'd been in, looked under tables and in toilet cubicles, quizzed bar staff, but all to no avail. Alas, he could not find his wallet anywhere.

It occurred to Matt that some kind-hearted soul might have handed his wallet in to the police, and he concluded the best course of action would be to pay a visit to the local koban. Near most Japanese train stations you can find a tiny koban- a wooden "police box" roughly the same size as a modest garden shed. The policemen inside spend their days giving street directions and recieving lost gloves and bus passes, (not exactly Miami Vice, then.) Surely Matt could rely on these dutiful public servants to help him?

Matt located a koban opposite the station, and proceeded to squeeze his bulky frame inside, smiling ingratiatingly at the two uniformed officers within. Unfortunately for him, the cops were extremely un-nerved by this unprecedented invasion. Upon seeing the vast, foreign beast-man, who had clearly been drinking, the cops became agitated and hostile. Before Matt could even open his mouth, the policemen demanded he show them some identification, namely the "alien registration card" that foreign nationals are required to carry at all times. This was a problem because the card was, of course, in his missing wallet. Matt tried to explain the situation in broken Japanese, but the two men couldn't understand his protestations.

They promptly arrested him. The policemen threw Matt into a cold cell for the night, without stopping to ponder the absurdity of an illegal immigrant voluntarily wandering into a police station. He languished there for several hours until he was finally able to get through to his slumbering roommate on his mobile phone, and beg him to get off the futon and bring his passport down to the police station, so that he could be released.

So, let's all give a big round of applause for the

Japanese Starskey and Hutch. Thanks to these brave and selfless heroes, a dangerous criminal was safely locked up behind bars, and the nation could sleep soundly once again.

Bottoms Up!

The following tale of sleaze and depravity takes place in the hedonistic seaside town of Enoshima, about an hour east of Tokyo. Danny and Jack, two high-school teachers no more emotionally mature than their students, had headed down there, hoping for some "spring break"-style hi-jinks during their summer vacation. One of the perks of being a schoolteacher in Japan is that you get the same, long holidays as the students.

Known as "the Miami Beach of Japan," Enoshima is a hot-spot for trendy youngsters, who hang out there all summer. The boys and girls of Tokyo go there to top up their tans, and party the night away in the wooden beach bars erected along the seafront.

Danny and Jack found themselves glugging on bottles of beer in one such beach bar, watching the sun set over the waves. As the nectar flowed they got friendly with the Japanese customers. Lots of cheesy chat-up lines, crowd-pleasing "wacky foreigner" antics and uproarious laughter ensued, as Jack and Danny wandered from table to table, paying particular attention to a group of holidaying office girls, who were equally as drunk and rambunctious as the two lecherous teachers.

These accommodating young ladies were still dressed for the beach, in bikinis and little else, so the boys were soon overheated, and the beer was doing little to dowse the flames of lust. The pair of them had red faces and bulging eyes like amphetamine-freaks, and were drooling like lobotomized babies.

Nonetheless, as the night progressed, Jack found himself getting along famously with one giggling, tan-skinned honey, appealingly clad in a pink bikini. He invited her for a stroll along the beach. The perfect setting for romance, he thought. As they wandered along the shore, talking, and admiring the stars reflected in the rippling ocean, he steeled himself to move in for a kiss.

"Do you have a condom?" the girl suddenly inquired. Jack was taken aback by her forwardness, but far from disappointed. His only qualm was that the answer to her question was 'no'.

"Do I have a condom with me now? er...No. Not as such... But I'm sure I can find one somewhere."

"No, that's OK. You'll just have to put your thing in the other hole instead."

Jack was shocked by this presumptuous proposition, since he'd only known the girl for about an hour, but the Corona flowing in his veins had dissolved his inhibitions and, after a day spent in the company of bikini-clad women, he now had desperate libido of Benny Hill on Viagra. He quickly yanked down his pants and got down to business.

Soon after, the deed was done and the pair of them returned to the beach bar to continue with the festivities. They separated and mingled, and a dazed Jack found himself necking another drink. Danny bounded over.

"Where have you been?" he enquired.

"You're not going to believe this." Jack garbled excitedly. "I just made love to that girl over there, on the beach!"

"Which one?"

"That one," he discreetly gestured towards the obliging lassie, who was now chatting innocently with her friends.

Danny stared at his friend in astonishment. "Her? You're kidding! I just shagged her in the arse about an hour ago!"

Jack's mouth slackened, and he looked at Danny in horror.

Who said romance was dead?

Fun at the VD Clinic

 All the indiscriminate hanky-panky that Eikaiwa teachers indulge in comes at a price, as Rich learned the hard way one morning, when he woke up with an unpleasant rash on his nether regions. Uh-oh.

Within a few days, his trousers housed a hellish mess of itchy inflammations and oozing yellow stuff, and he was reduced to limping around with a pained expression on his face. The poor fella was really paying for his promiscuity.

Rich glumly accepted that he would have to visit a VD clinic. This situation would have been embarrassing enough in his home country, but in a land famous for it's dignity and reserve, discussing sex-diseases and leaking genitals was sure to be supremely awkward. This situation would be further complicated by his babyish grasp of the Japanese language.

Rich swallowed his pride, phoned his company's head office and asked them to find an English-speaking doctor. Such a request was not uncommon, and Rich was thankful when he was given directions to a urology clinic near the school in which he worked.

The following morning, grimacing with discomfort, Rich waddled like a morose Charlie Chaplin into the clinic. He was gratified when the receptionist greeted him in English. The lack of language barriers would make the proceedings far less painful.

He sat in the sterile waiting room until an attractive nurse appeared, holding an empty plastic cup. She instructed him to go into the lavatory and fill the cup with pee for the doctor to examine. A firm believer in first impressions, Rich was rather abashed that such a stunning girl knew he was infected with an STD. Oh well, romance was unlikely to blossom in a VD clinic, anyway.

Rich urinated in the cup and handed it sheepishly to the nurse for analysis, then returned to the waiting area and sat, waiting anxiously for his results. After an hour the nurse returned and said "the doctor will see you now."

As he followed the nurse down the corridor, Rich was relieved that his mind would soon be put at rest. Hopefully he would be able to score some antibiotics to clear up the problem in his pants.

However, when the nurse ushered him into the doctor's office, Rich's sense of relief quickly evaporated. Sat behind a desk, about to inform him of the results of the test, was a man he recognized. Rich broke into a cold sweat as Doctor Watanabe, one of his adult students and the father of two children in Rich's kids classes, coldly diagnosed him with a dose of the clap.

Chin Chin

Although shouting "chin chin!" is a fine way to propose a toast in Italy, I have learned not to do so in Japan, since "chin chin" means "penis." Crying the word "penis!" before knocking back a drink can only lead to confusion, so I find it's best avoided. Anyway, drinks and dicks both have relevance to the following story.

Once, feeling sweaty and sluggish on my way home from a punishing all-night piss-up, I decided to make a pit stop at the convenience store near my home. Japanese "convenie"s are brightly-lit shrines to capitalism that can be found on every street corner, open all day and night, with inexplicable names like "Three F" and "Sunkus" (a woeful attempt to spell "thanks.") Inside, they look like compact versions of Willy Wonka's Chocolate Factory, full of shelves adorned with luminous packages and bottles branded with bewildering, boldly-written gibberish names like Pocky, Pocari Sweat, Asse, Calpis and Bubble Man II. You can buy comics, condoms, DVDs, make-up, batteries, lightbulbs, bananas and, most importantly, alcohol. But, that day, I was looking for something different.

In one corner of every Japanese convenience store is a small refrigerator full of tiny glass bottles known as "genki-drinks." Sickly chemical remedies for any ailment you can think of, from influenza to constipation, all there to make life more bearable for the pertinacious wage slaves who pop in and out at all hours. I wanted buy one of these little bottles of elixir, for I was in dire need of a hangover cure. I was due to leave for work in a couple of hours, and in my current condition I couldn't bear to sit in a classroom and face an endless succession of monotonous businessmen, housewives and pensioners. I was praying for a transformation akin to Popeye after gulping down a can-full of spinach.

In the convenie I couldn't decode the spidery Japanese characters on any of the genki-drink labels so, aching and desperate, I splashed out on the most expensive bottle, in the naive hope that, at that price, it must surely be super-effective at curing any problem. The bottle had a gold label and looked classy, as if it were "The King of Genki Drinks", so I was feeling optimistic.

Back in my living room I swallowed the concoction whole, screwing up my face at the bitter aftertaste. Disappointingly, the Popeye reaction didn't happen. If anything, I felt even more horribly nauseous than before.

A Japanese friend of my room-mate had been dozing on the sofa, and was woken by my retches of repulsion. As he rose from his slumber, yawning, he

spied the empty bottle in my hand and raised an eyebrow. "Why are you drinking that?"

"Eh?" I sensed I was in for some unwanted news. He laughingly informed me that it was a herbal potion for increasing the libido of old men. Much to my alarm, I was told the key ingredient in this witches' brew was powdered seal penis. Seal penis?! Can you believe they actually sell this unholy stuff in convenience stores? There must be a lot of pissed-off eunuch seals swimming around the coast of Japan.

I later arrived at work still feeling battered and dozy, but I was conspicuously alert in one department, as you can imagine. While I could barely stand up straight, my "chin chin" was standing to attention all day.

Closing Time

Alas, even for the most foolhardy of booze-guzzling gigolos, the party must come to an end at some point. The pleasure-seeker in Japan can only maintain the horseplay for so long before the novelty wears off. Some teachers fly home. Others, tamed by the sobering influence of a local lover, stay in Japan, adopt the native customs and start behaving themselves, perhaps finally getting around to achieving their original goals of learning martial arts or mastering the language, (but, more likely, they get cable TV and sit around watching The Cartoon Network a lot.)

I've been in this remarkable country for a long time now and I've gradually absorbed many of the Japanese ways. In fact, despite all my deplorable confessions, I'm a proper goody two-shoes these days. It took me well over a year to notice that I was the only one glugging beer on the train at six AM. Now I, myself, feel decidedly uneasy when I see noisy, belligerent Westerners sauntering towards me in train carriages. "Hypocrite"? Me?

Well, it's time to draw things to a close. I should emphasize once again that not all teachers in Japan are sex-crazed alkies. Indeed, some of the sweetest, most altruistic individuals I've met have been English teachers. There are a few good apples floating in the barrel of scum.

It's been quite a challenge to recall all the details of these tales through the mist of a thousand sake-related hangovers. I hope it's been an education for you. Sayonara!

Lightning Source UK Ltd.
Milton Keynes UK
15 January 2011

165766UK00001B/80/P